LEARN
THE LESSONS
OF
LIFE!

Birister Sharma

Copyright © 2022 Birister Sharma

All Rights Reserved.

Made with ♥on the Notion Press Platform

www.notionpress.com

Dedicated to my loving wife....

Pallabi Devi Sharma

I surrendered to you, O my Lord......

"Om Namah Shivaya"

Table of Contents

One word

Our life is like a long journey, and we all are like distant travelers. In every moment of our life's journey, we have to face many challenges and hurdles. But these challenges and hurdles teach us many amazing lessons in life and make us more learned and knowledgeable.

Life is like an open book. Every day is a new chapter and brings new lessons in our life. Every moment, we read and learn something. Every moment is an exciting and astonishing experience for us. We have no idea what will happen in the next moment of our life.

But every passing moment tells us something; every passing moment teaches us something; every passing moment guides us; and every passing moment enlightens us with some lesson, moral, wisdom, and knowledge.

However, we have to open the eyes of our mind, heart, and soul in order to read and learn.

1. Your curiosity

Your curiosity is the first step to learning something new in your life.

Your curiosity awakens you from the slumbering mind of your ignorance and darkness. Your curiosity is like the shining sunlight that disperses the dark clouds of doubt and unawareness from your life. It leads you to new doors of great wisdom and infinite knowledge.

Millions of people have seen the falling apple from the apple tree before Isaac Newton, but nobody was curious to know the cause of the falling apple only in the downward direction. It was only Isaac Newton who was so curious to know about the cause of the falling apple downward that he started asking questions to himself and discovered the famous 'Gravitational Law.'

You will only learn something new if you have curiosity in your mind, heart, and spirit. Allow your mind, heart, and spirit to learn something new.

Without curiosity, you will never learn or do anything in your life. See the small children; they are always curious to know everything. Whenever they are accompanied by their parents, they never stop asking questions. They put one question after another, non-stop. They have endless questions in their minds.

Always try to become like small children with a curious mind.

It is the curiosity of a man that has led him to discover or invent so many new things in this world that were impossible for him in his early days and years.

A man never becomes a scientist, inventor, discoverer, or researcher if he has no curiosity in his mind. Many people lack wisdom and knowledge because they have no curiosities in their minds. So, they never know or learn new things in their entire lives. They spend their lives in ignorance and darkness.

Where there is curiosity, there is wisdom and knowledge. Where there is no curiosity, there is only ignorance and darkness.

Your curiosity will direct you to new horizons. It inspires you to do something new in your life. It will unlock the door to every hidden wisdom and knowledge and every mystery of this world.

Curiosity is the only medium to unearth your hidden potential. When your curiosity develops within you, only then will you be able to utilize your natural skills and talents in constructive ways. You will also find new direction in your life.

It is the curiosity of a man to fly like the birds, so he invented a flying machine, which is called an aeroplane in modern times. It is the curiosity of a man to travel faster than a running horse, so he invented a high-horsepower vehicle.

Once you know your curiosity, you'll discover or invent anything in this world. Your curiosity will give you new wings to fly from the unknown to the known.

When your curiosity comes into your mind, you'll become desperate to know and to do something that is hidden from you. You want to discover or invent something new at any cost, and that is the beginning of new creations in your life and in your world.

Your curiosity will help you become the person you want to be in your life. Follow your curiosity and discover your true self. Your curiosity is the only way to lead you from the unknown to the known. Your curiosity will help you find the answer to every question in your life. Where there is no curiosity, there is no wisdom and no knowledge.

Your curiosity is the beginning of your great wisdom and infinite knowledge.

Your curiosity is the mother of your wisdom and knowledge. Always keep your curiosity alive in your life.

Contemplate yourself

The future belongs to the curious. The ones, who are not afraid to try it, explore it, poke at it, question it and turn it inside out.

Curiosity is the spark behind the spark of every great idea.

Curiosity keeps us moving forward, exploring, experimenting, opening new doors.

--Walt Disney

I have no special talent. I am only passionately curious.

---Albert Einstein

Curiosity is straight fire of creativity.

---Sam Harrison

2. *Perseverance*

It is not your skills and talents that make you successful in your life, but your tireless perseverance. Perseverance means never giving up before you achieve your cherished goal.

There is great power in your perseverance. You can achieve anything in your life with your sheer perseverance.

Perseverance turns the weak into the strong and the poor into the rich.

If you want to become a rich man in your life, then the only magic wand is your perseverance.

Rome is not built in a day. It was the perseverance of the people of Italy that built the magnificent city of Rome.

The Taj Mahal is not built in a day. It took twenty long years to complete the majestic building, and more than twenty thousand workers persevered day and night.

Perseverance makes everything possible in your life. Remember that "impossible" itself says, "I'm possible."

Your perseverance is the only key to your grand success.

A stonebreaker couldn't break a big boulder into small pieces with one small strike. But he has to strike continuously and tirelessly with his hammer, and finally, his one small strike is enough to break the big boulder into thousands of small pieces.

A river cannot cut through hard rock with its currents, but it can do so with continuous perseverance.

Your perseverance is priceless.

There is no measure of your perseverance.

Nothing is impossible for you if you persevere in your life.

Your perseverance is the key to your success.

You can only build your life with your perseverance.

Never be afraid of perseverance.

Your perseverance never kills you.

But it makes you strong and powerful.

Only your idleness and procrastination will kill you.

Be always aware of these bitter enemies of your success.

Your perseverance always pays you a grand price.

You can only build your majestic Taj Mahal with your sheer perseverance.

Your perseverance is the only way to fulfill every goal of your life.

Contemplate yourself

Great works are performed by not by strength but by perseverance.

---Samuel Johnson

A hero is an ordinary individual who finds the strength to persevere and endure in spite of overwhelming obstacles.

---Christopher Reeve

With ordinary talent and extraordinary perseverance, all things are attainable.

---Thomas Fowell Buxton

By perseverance the snail reached the ark.

---Charles Spurgeon

Perseverance is not a long race; it is many short races one after the other.

---Walter Elliot

3. *Focus*

Your past is dead; your present is just born. Therefore, don't weep for your past, but enjoy your present. Focus on your present moment and move ahead in your life.

Think in your present moment and plan in your present moment. Decide in your present moment. Act in your present moment. And live in your present moment.

Your present moment is precious for your life. Once it passes away from you, you will never regain it.

Utilize your present moment for constructive and creative work. It will help you gain something great in your coming days, coming weeks, coming months, and coming years. Don't waste your present moment on worthless things and unrewarding work.

Many people fail in their lives not because they lack skills and talents, but because they fail to utilize their present moment. Their main problem is their idleness and procrastination.

Your present moment is the golden period to sow the seeds of your work, not the moment for gossip and idleness.

The deeds of your present moment will decide the outcomes of your future.

The present moment is the mother of your future. Don't waste your present moment. Make your present moment productive.

Your success always depends on the perseverance of your present moment.

Make your present moment successful with your hard work and dedication. Don't worry about your future, because your future is the child of your present.

Focus on your present.

It is the golden moment to initiate something great in your life.

Never waste it.

Focus on your work.

Focus on your hard work and dedication.

Utilize your present moment in a constructive way.

Your future is always decided by the work you execute in your present.

Focus! Focus! Focus!

Only focus on your present moment!

Your focus on your present moment is the only path to your great happiness, success, prosperity, and peace.

Contemplate yourself

Regrets are wasted thoughts. Focus on the present.

Realize deeply that the present moment is all you have. Make the Now the primary focus of your life.

Do not dwell in the past. Do not dream of the future, concentrate the mind on the present moment.

---Lord Buddha

Forget the past that made you cry, and focus on the present that completes your smile.

Today's action is tomorrow's progress. Let go of the past, focus on your present and secure your future.

12

4. Your Imagination

You can imagine anything. Your imagination is the power of your mind. Your imagination consists of your mental images and pictures. If you imagine beautiful things, you will see beautiful things around you. If you imagine ugly things, you will see horrible things around you.

With your imagination, you can view what you want before you actually act in your reality.

Be careful before you imagine anything, because as you imagine, so you attain in your life.

If you imagine yourself as great, then you will become great in your life. It is your imagination that makes you the way you want to be. You are the by-product of your imagination.

You will become a winner if you imagine yourself a winner.

There is great power in your imagination. You can create anything with your imagination. A great painter always imagines great images and pictures before he paints his masterpiece. You are like a painter of your life. Imagine great images and pictures of your life, and then paint your life with beautiful images and colorful pictures.

Imagination gives you clear pictures of your life. It also provides you with a roadmap for your life. You have nothing to pay for your imagination.

Your imagination gives you the first instance to review yourself before you act on something and paves the way to analyze yourself thoroughly. Then you will easily measure your weak points and strong points before you execute something.

Your imagination is so powerful that you can imagine anything. You can make impossible things into possible things with your imagination.

One day, two pregnant women were admitted to the same hospital. The first woman imagined a beautiful image of her child right from the day she got pregnant, and she delivered a healthy and beautiful child. On the other hand, the second woman imagined an ugly image of her child right from the day she got pregnant, and she delivered an unhealthy and ugly child. This is how our imagination plays a crucial role in our lives. Clear your imagination to get clear images and pictures of your life.

Your imagination is a powerful tool to do great things and achieve great things.

If you imagine great, you will become great.

If you imagine grand success, you will attain your grand success.

Your imagination is a replica of your reality.

Therefore, be careful before you imagine anything, because the way you imagine yourself is the way you will become in your actual life.

Your imagination is the most powerful tool in your life, because with the power of your imagination, you can do anything.

A sculptor, before he carves any sculpture, imagines the image of the sculpture in his mind.

Contemplate yourself

Your imagination is your preview of life's coming attractions.

---Albert Einstein

Your imagination is the weapon of mass construction. Use it.

You can't depend on your eyes when your imagination is out of focus.

---Mark Twain

Worry is a misuse of your imagination.

Your imagination is the hood ornament on the car of creativity.

---Gary Busey

You're limited only by your imagination.

---Benny Bellamacina

5. Mistakes

Never be scared to commit mistakes. Only your mistakes will teach you about the great lessons of life.

Mis + Take → Mistake

Mistake means if you miss something by chance, then you can take it once again.

There is nobody who doesn't make mistakes in their life. Everybody makes mistakes in their life. But you have every right to correct your mistakes.

Always keep an eraser along with your pencil.

A mistake means to learn something new. If you are making mistakes in your work, it means you are learning something new in your life.

We never learn anything without making mistakes. Our mistakes are a part of our learning experience. Your mistakes will make you wiser and more intelligent. Your mistakes make you a better person and perfect you in your life. In other words, your mistakes will give you new opportunities to improve yourself.

Thomas Alva Edison made a thousand mistakes when he experimented in his lab, and later everything became history. He invented the electric bulb. In every mistake, Thomas Alva Edison learned new ways to make an electric bulb.

Make mistakes to do something great, but not to harm anything or anybody. If you are making mistakes while doing your work, then they are not your mistakes; they are your constructive way to improve yourself. They will always lead you toward the door of success.

On the contrary, if you are making mistakes with the intention to destroy something or somebody, then it is not your mistake; it is a pre-planned destructive way to commit a crime. It will always lead you to the ditch of hell.

If you make mistakes, then you will know what is going wrong with you. You can review your mistakes and improve yourself. Accept your mistakes gladly, and amend your mistakes straight away the moment you realize them. But never leave them. Because your one small mistake can become a dangerous thing for you; it may spoil everything in your life. Always remember that you never learn anything without making mistakes. You have learned to walk while falling down many times. You have learned to speak while stammering many times. You have learned your handwriting while you scrambled the alphabets many times.

Never care about what other people will say about you if you make any mistakes while executing your work. Just do your work. Forget everything.

Many people think about what other people will say about us if we make any mistakes. This "What will other people say about us?" is the major problem that blocks us from doing something new and great in our lives.

You will never achieve great success if you never make mistakes in your life. Your mistakes will teach you and guide you about the causes of your shortcomings and open a new door to your self-improvement.

Therefore, always observe your mistakes and try to figure them out. Ask yourself if you feel any doubt in your mind. Then you'll know your mistakes and their correct solutions.

Behind every successful day, there are many countless mistakes in one's life.

Mistakes are a part of your life. Accept them with your bright smile and gratitude.

Never be scared of your mistakes.

Your mistakes are your great teachers.

They will teach you many valuable lessons about your life.

You will never learn anything if you never make mistakes.

Your mistakes will make you strong.

Your mistakes will help you unclutter your latent mind.

Your mistakes will open new doors of opportunities.

Only through your mistakes can you discover new things.

There is nobody in this world who has never made any mistakes.

Learn from your mistakes.

But never repeat the same mistakes.

Correct them straight away before you proceed further.

Mistakes are your best friends if you know how to gain wisdom and knowledge from them.

Never be afraid of your mistakes. A man who never commits any mistakes will never learn anything in his life. Your mistakes will make you mature and experienced. Your mistakes will give you another opportunity to improve yourself.

Contemplate yourself

A person who never made a mistake, he never tried anything new.

---Albert Einstein

Mistakes have the power to turn you into something better than you were before.

21

The biggest mistake you can ever make is being afraid to make one.

Failure is the key to success; each mistake teaches us something.

---Morihei Ueshiba

Making mistakes is better than faking perfections.

6. Live in the present

Tomorrow never comes in your life. Time and tide never wait for anybody. Therefore, live your life in your present moment.

What you can do today, you will never do tomorrow. Today is in your hands. You can do anything now, and today. If you rely on and depend on tomorrow, then you will never accomplish anything worthwhile in your life.

Never depend on tomorrow. Depend on your today.

Never leave anything for tomorrow. Think in your present moment. See your dream in your present moment. Aim in your present moment. Make your plan in your present moment. Make your decision in your present moment. Prepare yourself in your present moment. Do your work in your present moment. Make your present moment your golden moment.

Live your life in your present moment. Never live your life in your past moment. Your present moment is your life, but your past moment is already dead. If you want to be happy and content in your life, then always live your life in your present moment, because your present moment is the foundation of your great future.

Your past is already gone. It is like your canceled check. Your present moment is in your hands. It is your cash. Spend it now. Enjoy it. Your future is still out of your sight, so don't worry about it. Concentrate only on your present moment.

Don't waste your present moment on gossip and criticism. Enjoy your present moment with your innovative ideas, constructive, and creative work. It will enrich your life and build your world.

Your success always depends on your present moment. The way you build your present moment is the way your future will be built.

All the successful men and women in this world are the builders of their present moments because they know very well that if they build their present moments, then only will their futures shine brightly.

If you have any commitments to execute, then do them in your present moment. Don't postpone them for tomorrow, the coming days, the coming weeks, or the coming years. Do it right now. Today. Because you have no idea what will happen tomorrow or in your coming days, weeks, months, or years. Your present moment is very precious to you. Everything is decided by whatever you think and do in your present moment.

Why are some people happy and successful? And why are some people unhappy and unsuccessful in their lives? The main reason is that those people who are happy and successful are fully focused on their present lives; they have no time to look back at their past lives, and they have no time to worry about their futures either. They are just enjoying their present moments. They are too busy making their present moments successful and glorious.

On the other hand, those people who are unhappy and unsuccessful in their lives are always recalling and reliving their past lives and worrying about their futures. They are just repenting and neglecting their glorious present moments. They are too busy spending their present moments on superfluous things.

Focus on your present moment, and do what is right for you and what is important for you.

What do you want in your life?

A happy life or an unhappy life?

Where do you want to live your life?

In your present moment or in your past moment?

Ask yourself and decide what you exactly want in your life and where you want to see yourself.

Your present moment is like your present wife or your present husband or your present girlfriend or your present boyfriend.

Your past is like your ex-wife or your ex-husband or your ex-girlfriend or your ex-boyfriend.

Who will give you more happiness and pleasure in your present life?

Your present wife or your ex-wife; your present husband or your ex-husband; your present girlfriend or your ex-girlfriend; your present boyfriend or your ex-boyfriend?

The decision is always yours. You have to decide for yourself.

If you make your present moment secure and successful, then your future will automatically become secure and successful. You have nothing to worry about. Therefore, make your present moment secure and successful.

Once upon a time, two best friends from a village went to work in a distant town. They worked and lived together for many years. The first friend was very smart in managing his wealth, so whatever he earned, he spent half of his earnings on living and invested the other half in purposeful business. On the other hand, the second friend only spent his earnings on living and merry-making. He never cared about his present moment. He had an ideology of "Let's see tomorrow." Therefore, he had neither saved his money nor invested it in any purposeful business.

After ten years, a financial breakdown occurred in the entire town. There were no more sources of income left for livelihood. Many people were becoming jobless and wandering for work. In that crucial time, the first friend became financially sound and secure; he had set up his own business in the same town with his savings and invested money.

However, the second friend was struggling for every single penny; he had no work and no money. He had no other option left but to leave the town. So he went back to his village empty-handed.

What is the moral of the story?

The moral of the story is: save and invest whatever you have in your present moment, because you never know when the tides of time will turn against you.

As you secure your present moment, you secure your future.

Because your future is directly proportional to your present moment.

Life is very short and full of mysteries. Nobody knows, and nobody predicts what will happen next. Therefore, live your life in your present moment with full planning and preparation. If you want to do your work, then do it in your present moment. If you want happiness and joy in your life, then enjoy your present moment. If you want to love your beloved ones, then love them in your present moment. If you want something special, then make your present moment special. If you want to give something to your dear ones, then give it to them in your present moment. If you want to forgive someone, then forgive them in your present moment. If you want to live your life fully, then live your life in your present moment. Never leave anything for tomorrow. Do it right now. Do it today. Love yourself and love your present moment. Make your present moment a special and glorious moment, and move ahead in your life while keeping your hopes and smiles alive.

Live in your present moment.

Focus on your present moment.

Never waste it.

Utilize it.

Think in your present moment.

Plan in your present moment.

Decide in your present moment.

Work in your present moment.

Enjoy in your present moment.

Make it special for you.

Make it successful for you.

Your life is always decided by your present moment.

Everything is in the hands of your present moment.

Live your life in your present moment.

Never leave anything for tomorrow.

Your present moment is your life.

Your present moment is your world.

You can do anything in your present moment.

What you can do in your present moment, you can't do once it slips away from your hands.

Your present moment is your life. Your past is your graveyard, which is already buried. And your future is not yet born; it is inside the womb of your present moment.

You have nothing to worry about. Just concentrate on your present moment.

Your grand success is always waiting for you.

Contemplate yourself

The point of power is always in the present moment.

---Louise L Hay

Wherever you are, be there. If you can be fully present now, you'll know what it means to live.

---Steve Goodier

Nothing is precious than being in the present moment. Fully alive, fully aware.

---Thich Nhat Hanh

The art of life is to live in the present moment.

---Emmet Fox

Happiness is not something you postpone for the future; it is something you design for the present.

---Jim Rohn

7. Create your value

Create your own value. There is nothing more valuable than your own life. Love your life. Care for your life. Enrich your life. Grow your life. Develop your life. Make your life meaningful and purposeful.

Make your life valuable like a precious gem. Polish your life every day with good thoughts, good ideas, good knowledge, good lessons, good experiences, good plans, good decisions, and good executions. When gold is mined from the goldmine, it is in an impure state, which means it is in its natural state, but when it is polished, it starts shining and glazing, and it becomes valuable. In the same fashion, you will never shine and become valuable in your life until you polish yourself.

Nobody will care about you if you do not care about yourself. You are valuable to yourself. If you care for yourself, it means you value yourself. And if you value yourself, it means you love and care for yourself. Never expect that someone will value you. If you think that someone will give you value, then you are making a fool of yourself. You have to value yourself. You have to make yourself valuable with your great deeds. Always keep in mind that you are the most valuable person in your life.

Give value to your loved ones, parents, family members, friends, colleagues, and neighbors. Giving value to others means you not only love and care about yourself, but you also love and care for them. If you give them value, then only will they give you the same value. Value gives value. Everything runs under the principle of give and take.

Life is always give and take.

Give value to your health; never take it for granted. Your health is the biggest asset in this world. Avoid bad habits such as smoking, alcohol, drugs, and anything that is injurious to your health.

Why do so many people suffer from serious health problems in their lives? The main reason is their negligence of their health. They never adopt the right food habits and fail to maintain a balanced diet. They have forgotten that their health is their biggest wealth and that it is under their control. However, they are so busy in their day-to-day lives that they take everything casually. They have a silly excuse: "We have no time to maintain our health. We are very busy with our work." If they have a mild headache, they will take a painkiller. If they experience minor chest pain, back pain, or any kind of body pain, they tend to take it for granted. They have no time for any medical check-ups. They have a mindset that once everything is settled down in their lives, then they will maintain their health. But they have failed to notice that their bodies are indicating something related to their health issues. By the time everything is about to settle down in their lives, it will be too late for them to cure their health. Then, whatever they have earned in their lives, they will have to spend on curing their health, but unfortunately, their huge sums of wealth will not cure their health.

As you treat your health, so your health treats you back.

Give value to your job. It is your source of earning and living. Never neglect your job. Love it and enjoy it fully, no matter how much you earn from it, and no matter the size of your job. Just do your best. Give your one hundred percent effort and dedication to your job. Every job is important in this world. The size of a job is never measured, but its value is always measured. Always feel proud of your job. If you are able to serve at least one percent of society through your job, then it is a great achievement in your life.

Give value to your habits. Cultivate good habits. They will enrich your life. Your good habits are your best pals; they will always guide you toward a good life. Avoid your bad habits. They will spoil your life. Your bad habits are like your worst company. They will ruin your beautiful life and make your world hell.

Control your habits, but never be controlled by them. Be the master of your good habits, but never be a slave to your bad habits.

One good habit will build your life, while one bad habit will destroy it. Therefore, beware of your bad habits and quit them as soon as possible before they swallow you completely.

Give value to your character. Your character is the identity of your true self. Nurture good character in your life and take care of it. Your character is like a white paper; everything is visible on it. You can write whatever you want on it. Your character is the true certificate of your life. Never allow it to be lost anywhere. Protect it and save it.

If something is lost, nothing is lost.

If health is lost, something is lost.

If character is lost, everything is lost.

Give value to your relationships. Your good relationships with anybody, whether with your spouse, family members, friends, neighbours, or colleagues, are very significant in your life. Without good relationships, you couldn't live your life happily and peacefully.

Think for a moment: if you have a bad relationship with your spouse, can you live happily in your house?

No.

If you have a bad relationship with your family members, can you live together in your house?

No.

If you have a bad relationship with your friends, can you maintain a good friendship?

No.

If you have a bad relationship with your neighbours, can you live together in your society?

No.

If you have a bad relationship with your colleagues, can you work together in your office or in your workplace?

No.

Give value to everybody and everything.

Give value to your personality. Your personality is very significant for you because it discloses many things about you: the way you perceive things, the way you think, the way you see, the way you communicate, the way you behave, and the way you live your life. Your personality is the outlook of your inner self.

How can you make yourself valuable in your life? It always depends on you. Coal, gold, and diamond—all these three materials are made of carbon products, but their values are different.

So the question that arises here is: what do you want to become in your life? Like coal, or like gold, or like diamond? You have to choose for yourself and create your own value. Nobody can create your value; it is only you who can create your value.

Create your own value.

Your life is the most valuable thing in this world.

You will become the way you give value to yourself.

Love yourself.

Care for yourself.

Make yourself like a precious jewel.

You are the maker of your own life and world.

Give value to yourself.

Give value to everybody.

You are the first person to value yourself.

Nobody will value you if you can't value yourself.

There is nothing more valuable than your life. Love your life. Care for your life. Enrich your life. Grow your life. Develop your life.

Make your life meaningful and purposeful. Live your life fully.

Make your life a complete package of love, happiness, success, prosperity, and peace.

Contemplate yourself

Your value doesn't decrease based on someone's inability to see your worth.

If you find yourself constantly trying to prove your worth to someone, you have already forgotten your value.

Self respect, self worth and self love, all start with self. Stop looking outside of yourself for your value.

---Rob Liano

If someone doesn't see your value and doesn't treat you right, then that person is worth-less to you, not the other way around.

---Jenna Ryan

The value of a person is measured by his self worth.

8. Don't expect different results

You don't get anything if you don't work in your life. Your mere expectation doesn't give you any results. If you expect something in your life, then you have to execute your work the way you expect. The more you expect in your life, the harder you have to work; only then will your expectations turn into actual results.

If you grow flowering plants in your garden, you will always get flowers. You can't expect fruits from flowering plants. Have you ever seen a rose flower in a thorny bush? You will never see a rose flower in a thorny bush. You will always see thorns in a thorny bush, and you will always see a rose flower on a rose plant. These are the natural order and law.

In a similar way, your life is shaped by how you work; the way you work in your life is the way you will get results. It is never possible that you have worked in one particular area and are expecting ten different results from it. You will never get anything. You are just wasting your precious time and misleading yourself.

You will always get one result from one piece of work. Your life is not a fictional drama or any fairy tale where many things occur at one time and in one place simultaneously. Your life always depends on practical execution and work.

As you sow, so shall you reap. This is the universal truth.

In a small town, two families lived nearby. The first family belonged to an educated background, so they treated their children lovingly and respectfully from an early age. When their children grew up and were well settled, they also treated their parents in the same manner, with love and respect, as they had been treated in their earlier days.

On the other hand, the second family was completely different. They treated their children harshly and poorly. So when their children grew up, they too treated their parents in the same manner, harshly and poorly.

In your life, you will always find that whatever you do, everything reflects back to you. It is like the reflection of a mirror. Therefore, always be careful about whatever you do in your life.

If you do good deeds, in return you will gain good results in your life. A hero is always honored by the people for his heroic deeds. But a villain is always disgraced by the people and punished by the law for his vice. When a thief is caught, he will always receive punishment for his crime, but he will not receive rewards.

Your life will always give you rewards if you do good deeds. If you hate somebody and expect love from him, it is foolishness. You will never receive love in return for hatred from him. Love leads to love. Hatred leads to hatred.

Good things lead to good things and good results.

Bad things lead to bad things and bad results.

If you give happiness to your loved ones—your spouse, your children, your parents, your relatives, your friends, your neighbors, and your colleagues—you will always receive happiness in return. And it will increase your joy and happiness.

Life always depends on give and take.

The way you give is the way you will get.

You will never receive anything while giving nothing.

It is like "no pain, no gain."

If you work hard to achieve great success in your life, you will definitely achieve your great success, no matter how many tough situations try to knock you down from your path to success. Your hard work will always pay you fruitful results in the end.

In the winter season, you will never expect mangoes. And in the summer season, you will never expect oranges. If you want to relish mango juice, then you will have to wait for the summer season. And in the same way, if you want to taste sweet oranges, then you will have to wait for the winter season.

In a similar way, our life is like a season; sometimes it is like the happiness of spring, and sometimes it is like the sorrow of autumn. But in every season of our life, we get different tastes and flavors.

Never expect anything good if you are not doing good things in your life. If you do good things in your life, then you will definitely get good results. On the other hand, if you do bad things in your life, then you will get bad results for sure. There is no doubt about it.

Always remember this simple philosophy:

Be good; do good.

You will always be happy and content.

If you want good results in your life, then first of all, you have to do good work. Only then will your life respond to you and give you good results while multiplying your happiness and gratification.

The more you give, the more you get.

The less you give, the less you get.

It is like investing your money in a good business; the more you invest, the more returns you get, and conversely, the less you invest, the fewer returns you get.

Never make a fool of yourself in your life while expecting great results without giving one hundred percent effort in your work.

Never expect different results in your life.

You will get what you give.

You will get what is deserved for you.

If you deliver good work, you will get good results.

This is the real philosophy of life: give and take.

No work, no result.

No pain, no gain.

You will only get one result at a time.

You will never get different results from one piece of
work.

*The seeds of good always germinate good
plants. The seeds of bad always germinate bad
plants.*

*You should never expect good fruits from
bad seeds.*

You'll receive what you give in your life.

*You'll never expect different results from
one piece of work.*

This is the law of life.

Contemplate yourself

Don't expect different results if your habits are the same.

Everything in your life is a reflection of a choice you have made. If you want a different result, make a different choice.

When someone is so sweet to you, don't expect that person will be like that all the time. Remember, even the sweetest chocolate expires.

Don't expect too much, let everything flow.

If you expect the world to be fair with you because you are fair with them, it is like expecting a lion not to eat you because you don't eat lion!

9. Experience

Your experience is the biggest teacher in your life. Like a teacher teaches you about the lessons that are in the textbook, in the same way, your experience will teach you about the lessons of life.

You will learn from your experience. Your experience will teach you about both happiness and sorrow; both success and failure; both love and hatred; both right and wrong; and both life and death.

Your experience makes you a wiser and more knowledgeable person. Your experience increases your wisdom and knowledge. You'll become a refined man. You'll know everything in advance.

Your experience makes you more mature. When you gain experience in life, you'll become cool, calm, and down to earth. You'll never make any hasty or nasty decisions in your life. You can make your life well-balanced and composed.

An experienced sailor always knows how to handle his ship in furious sea storms. In the same way, an experienced man always knows how to handle himself in the tough situations of life. Your experience always guides you in your life. When you gain a lot of experience in your life, you will know how to guide yourself when you stray from the right direction.

Your experience is your biggest asset. Your experience will lead you to the path of great success even when there is no possibility of any success. Your experience will boost you up whenever there is a challenge in your life.

If you are experienced, then you have nothing to worry about in your life. Your experience will help you find your name and glory. Your experience will solve every problem in your life.

I have watched the Hindi movie 'Avataar' starring the first Bollywood superstar, Rajesh Khanna, more than five times. Every time I watch that movie, I learn a new lesson, moral, wisdom, and knowledge from it.

In the movie, Rajesh Khanna plays the role of a motor mechanic named Avataar Kishen. With the profession of a simple motor mechanic, he manages his family very well. He has two sons, and he educated both of them in a reputed college. He has an assistant named Savek, played by Sachin (a Bollywood hero), who is like his own son.

When his two sons are well established in their lives, one day, they forcefully deport Avataar Kishen and his wife, Radha, along with Savek. But Avataar Kishen accepts everything; he is not worried about anything.

He said firmly while comforting his weeping wife, "Radha, I have my experience. You have nothing to worry about. If I get my mechanical tools, then I will change the whole course of our lives."

Then, with his experience, Avataar Kishen changed everything; he invented a new formula to increase the RPM

(Revolutions per Minute) of a motor car. After a few years, he got a huge contract and built his own industry.

This movie teaches us that if we have experience in our respective fields, then we have nothing to worry about; we can do anything in our lives, no matter what hard circumstances try to knock us down.

Your experience never makes you a failure. Your experience will make you aware of your strong points and weak points. Your experience will prepare you before you undertake anything in your hands. Your experience will act as your third eye. You'll know everything that would happen in the next moment in your life.

Do you ever think about why a team in any sport needs an experienced coach? A team needs an experienced coach because only an experienced coach will be able to teach, guide, prepare, manage, handle, and train every player well. An experienced coach has already come across many tough and challenging moments in every game. He knows every game plan and every tactic of a game. He knows how to handle the pressure of the game; he knows the winning mantras; and he also knows how to bounce back from the bitter losses of the game.

You can teach, guide, prepare, manage, handle, and train yourself when you gain experiences in your life like an experienced coach.

Try to become an experienced coach of your own life.

Your experience makes you responsible in your life. Your experience makes you realize your responsibilities towards yourself, your goals, your work, your family, and your society.

Your experience plays an important role in your success. It will always motivate you to excel in your life. Your experience is the storehouse of wisdom and knowledge. Without experience, you'll never truly live in this world.

Never hesitate to gain experience in your life.

Your experience is the source of great knowledge.

Your experience never goes to waste.

Your experience will help you live your life fully.

Your experience is your greatest teacher.

Your experience is your greatest guide.

Your experience is your pathfinder.

Only your experience will solve your problems.

Your experience makes you fearless.

Your experience will lead you to great success.

Your experience is the biggest teacher in your life. Like a teacher teaches you about the lessons in the textbook, in the same way, your experience will teach you about the great lessons of life.

Contemplate yourself

Knowledge comes with experience, experience comes with lesson learned, and lesson learned comes with mistake.

---Ruskin Kwofie

The only source of knowledge is experience.

---Albert Einstein

Knowledge comes from learning. Experience comes from living. A life without problems is like a school without lessons. Keep walking with a positive mind.

The pebbles of knowledge must be bonded together by the cement of experience.

---R. G. Letourneau

The period of greatest gain in knowledge and experience is the most difficult period in one's life.

---Dalai Lama

47

10. Learn the rules

Learn the rules of life. Then live your life happily and peacefully. Life is not always easy. You'll never find your bed of roses so easily. In order to gain anything in your life, you've to resist pain initially. Only then will you gain something worthwhile in your life. The rule of life is no pain, no gain. You've to pay for something in order to get something in return.

Learn the rules to live. Always try to live a simple life with high thinking. Never try to make your life complex. Many people are unhappy because they always try to make their lives complex. In fact, they are not happy with their simple lives. But they have forgotten that there is a great beauty in a simple life. Try to live a simple life; you'll always be happy and content.

Leave the habits of complexity.

Develop the habits of simplicity.

Learn the rules to do your work. Do your work that is good for you. Do your work that suits you. Do your work that you like the most. Do your work that you enjoy the most. Do your work that you love the most. Don't try to do any work that is against you. Always do one task at a time. Don't try to do too many tasks in one go. You'll get confused in your work, and you'll never complete your work on time. And never postpone your work that you could do today. Do your work now. Do your work today. And love your work like you love your loved ones.

Learn the rules of creativity. Everywhere you need some creativity in order to give your work a final touch. Creativity is simply a new thought, a new idea, a new move, and a new step. Your creativity will reshape your life and rekindle your work as well as your world.

Learn the rules of happiness. Happiness is always within you. The more you give happiness to others, the more you receive happiness in your life. Your happiness will double if you learn to give happiness to other people. Don't look for your happiness in the outside world; look within yourself. Don't try to chase your happiness; you'll never catch it, because your happiness is just like a flying butterfly: the more you try to catch it, the more it'll fly away from you. Your happiness is just like a jewel around your neck; you'll always find it very close to you.

Learn the rules of peace. You will never find your peace anywhere in this world. You'll only find your peace within you. You'll never find your peace in the lives of other people. You'll only find your peace in your life.

Your peace is always dwelling inside you; you just need to look for it within yourself. If you want ultimate peace in your life, then give up your hatreds, give up your egos, give up your angers, give up your jealousies, give up your attachments, and give up your lust for material needs.

Learn the rules of contentment. A life without contentment is like a hellish life. Your contentment is your biggest inner wealth. Whatever you do in your life, whatever you achieve in your life, wherever you live your life, if you have no self-contentment, your life will become worthless and meaningless.

Learn the rules of love. There are no rules of love because love itself is its own rule. Love is the mother of everything. Where there is love, there is happiness, joy, peace, prosperity, unity, respect, understanding, honesty, compassion, and acknowledgment.

Love is the only rule to live your life in complete tranquility. The whole world is a composition of love. Our life is never possible without love. If you know how to love yourself and other people, then you don't need to know anything in this world, because your love will teach you and guide you in everything. With your love, you'll conquer this entire world. Love is the only language that doesn't need any words, sentences, or speeches to express, because love will express everything itself.

Learn the rules of compassion. Compassion brings you sympathy, concern, kindness, and care in your life. Without compassion, you can't live your life. Your compassion is the breath of your life. Always keep the fresh air of your compassion. If you want a happy and content life, then be compassionate with yourself and other people.

Learn the rules of success. The rules of success are a combination of your thoughts, your dreams, your ideas, your lessons, your wisdom, your knowledge, your aims and objectives, your plans, your decisions, your responsibilities, your habits, your attitudes, your courage, your potential, your energy and power, your enthusiasm, your balanced mind, your discipline, your self-belief, your self-confidence, your self-esteem, your acceptance, your contentment, your sacrifices, your challenges, your perseverance, your persistence, and your hard work.

Follow these rules of success; you'll reach the zenith of every triumph.

Never play the game of your life if you don't know its rules.

Learn the rules of your life.

Be the master of your life's rules.

You'll win any battle.

No Himalayan task will ever halt you from the path of your success.

Nobody will dare to defeat you.

You'll become an unbeatable warrior in your life.

You'll become like the king of this world.

If you suppose that your life is a game, then you've got to learn its every rule in order to play your game and break its rules, and you will make your own rules later on.

Contemplate yourself

You have to learn the rules of the game. And then you have to play better than anyone else.

---Albert Einstein

To learn who rules over you, simply find out who you are not allowed to criticize.

---Voltaire

Life is short. Break the RULES. FORGIVE quickly, KISS slowly, LOVE truly, LAUGH uncontrollably, and NEVER REGRET anything that made you smiles.

I follow three rules: Do the right thing, do the best you can, and always show people you care.

---Lou Holtz

Learn and obey the rules very well so you will know how to break them properly.

---Dalai Lama

About the author:

Birister Sharma is a full time author. He is also an avid reader. He loves reading, writing, and motivation. He has penned down dozens of self-help motivational books and novels so far.

You may contact him @ birister2007@gmail.com

www.ingramcontent.com/pod-product-compliance
Lightning Source LLC
Chambersburg PA
CBHW040201160726
48006CB00014B/1850